PRAYER
A Book

❖❖❖❖❖❖❖❖❖❖❖❖

JIM COTTER

SHEFFIELD
CAIRNS PUBLICATIONS
1989

© Copyright by Jim Cotter 1987, 1989
ISBN 1 870652 05 3

First published April 1987
Second edition May 1989

Further copies of this book are obtainable from
Cairns Publications
47 Firth Park Avenue, Sheffield S5 6HF

Printed by J. W. Northend Ltd
Clyde Road, Sheffield S8 0TZ

SEQUENCE

- v Introduction
- vi Notes and Acknowledgments
- 1 Sunday
- 11 Monday
- 21 Tuesday
- 31 Wednesday
- 41 Thursday
- 51 Friday
- 61 Saturday

INTRODUCTION

Prayer in the Day: A Book of Mysteries has been compiled as a companion volume to *Prayer at Night: A Book for the Darkness* and *Prayer in the Morning: A Book for Day's Beginning*. It can be used either by individuals or in groups, whenever there is ten or fifteen minutes available during the day. It has a simple structure:

> Introduction and Hymn
> Part of Psalm 119
> Themes for Meditation
> Prayers

The sequence is arranged according to the day of the week.

If the prayer is used corporately, it may be found appropriate for the whole company to say those parts which have a vertical line by them in the margin. Some of the prayers could be divided among several voices.

There is also a standard version of the book which has a series of line drawings as part of the meditations. These, together with a short prose-poem, were produced by the artist Peter Pelz. In this pocket edition there are quotations from the Bible which may help to create a mental picture for meditation.

The compiler has many people to thank, not least those known and unknown shapers of prayer whose pictures and words have been an inspiration and who in their time found fresh forms for new occasions. I hope that the Spirit in which they prayed and created has not been betrayed in these pages.

Particular thanks are due to Peter Jessop and Tim Day for their help with the tune *Welham Green*.

JIM COTTER
April 1989

NOTES AND ACKNOWLEDGMENTS

HYMNS

These are but suggestions: appropriate hymns are legion.

SUNDAY: by Edmund Spenser (1553–99); English Hymnal 283; tune: Farley Castle (10.10.10.10).

MONDAY: by John Mason (c. 1645–94); Hymns and Psalms 8; tune: Soll's Sein (D.C.M.).

TUESDAY: by the compiler; tune: Marching (8.7.8.7).

WEDNESDAY: by the compiler (the quotation at the head is by Henry Vaughan (1622–95); tune: any flowing melody, of which the following is no more than something the compiler found himself humming, and which he had no musical ability to transcribe without the help of more musical friends (who, it must be said, are not responsible for it).

THURSDAY: by Prudentius (b.348); English Hymnal 613, adapted by the compiler; tune: Divinum Mysterium (8.7.8.7.8.7.7).

FRIDAY: by Venantius Fortunatus (530–609), variously

translated; adapted by the compiler; English Hymnal 95 & 96, Hymns Ancient and Modern Revised 97; tune: Pange Lingua or French Carol (8.7.8.7.8.7).

SATURDAY: by George Herbert (1593–1633); Hymns and Psalms 254; tune: Come my Way (7.7.7.7).

PSALM

Each day has three sections of Psalm 119 (Sunday has four). These have been paraphrased, since in modern usage the words more accurately translated 'precepts', 'statutes', 'ordinances', have more legalistic associations than in the original Hebrew. They have been replaced by such words as 'counsel', 'wisdom', and 'way'. In Hebrew these are closely associated with the words 'Torah' and 'Law', understood as the gift of a gracious God to the People of Israel. Thus an attempt has been made to express the spirit of the original psalm, a spirit which is more in tune with Christian thought than might be imagined from an initial reading.

Each section has also been given a heading (no more than an indicator) and certain 'prompts', so linking the psalm both to stages of our pilgrimage in God and also to passages from the Gospels. For the 'Law' may be thought of as invitation and implication consequent on our acceptance of the incredible gift of the love of God into our lives, rather than detailed prescriptions that can so easily turn religious practice into moralising burden. The 'invitations' are drawn from the Gospel according to John, the 'implications' from the other three Gospels.

MEDITATIONS

The arrangement of the meditations bears some resemblance to the traditional 'mysteries' of the Gospel, prayed with the aid of the Rosary. No more than one of these is suggested as a focus on any one day: if they are used regularly the whole sequence covers a ten week period. For convenience the words of the

'Hail Mary' and of an alternative are printed at the beginning of the 'Prayers' for each day. The repetition of the words act as a background murmur to still the restless intellect and help the mind and heart and will to focus on the chosen 'mystery'.

The sources of the biblical passages are:

SUNDAY: Genesis 1.2; Mark 16.2–6; Acts 1.9; Acts 2.2–3; Romans 8.18–21; Genesis 32.24–31; Revelation 2.17; Isaiah 53.7; Isaiah 11.9; Genesis 28.10–22.

MONDAY: Luke 1.26–38; 1.39–44; 2.7; 2.34–35; 2.49–52; Isaiah 44.23; Matthew 6.28–29; Psalm 104.16–17; 104.25–26; Genesis 12.16.

TUESDAY: Hosea 11.3–4; Matthew 26.10–12; Romans 8.29; 1 Corinthians 15.45, 49; Song of Songs 2.10–12; Hebrews 2.10; Mark 8.25; Isaiah 53.5; Colossians 2.9; Exodus 3.14 and John 8.58.

WEDNESDAY: Mark 2.4, 5, 11; Luke 7.2, 6, 7, 9; 8.44, 46, 47; 17.12–16; Mark 7.25–30; John 5.2–9; Mark 3.31–35; John 4.7–30; Luke 19.1–10; 10.25–37.

THURSDAY: Matthew 3.13–17; 4.1–11; 17.1–8; 26.12; 26.20–29; Luke 2.16–19; Mark 14.66–72; Mark 1.19–20; John 13.21–30; John 11.43–44.

FRIDAY: Mark 14.32–42; John 19.1; 19.2–3; 19.17; Mark 15.33–37; Revelation 1.16 and Luke 22.36; Isaiah 24.1, 4; Jeremiah 4.4; Mark 13.2; Isaiah 58.4.

SATURDAY: John 15.5; 4.14; 6.35; 8.1; 11.25; Mark 11.15–19; John 11.34–36; Luke 22.44; Mark 10.17–22; Luke 15.23–24.

PRAYERS

SUNDAY: An affirmation, addressed to God in Christ, focusing on the Easter Gospel, and using Hebrew names: Yeshua (Joshua), Ruach (Spirit), Yahweh (Jehovah).

MONDAY: A version of the Lord's Prayer inspired by various reflections of Louis Evely in his book *Our Father*, Mowbray, 1970, with gratitude for the original stimulus.

TUESDAY: The prayer on p.28 can be used with bodily gestures.

That on p.29 is a simplified adaptation of a way of praying of the Buddhist tradition, introduced to me first through George Appleton's book, *One Man's Prayers*, SPCK, 1967. I should wish to acknowledge my gratitude for this.

WEDNESDAY: A version of the Lord's Prayer by the compiler, using the Indian word 'Bapu' for 'Father', a word that carries overtones of deep respect and regard as well as of close intimacy. It can be prayed in tune with breathing, each phrase being spoken slowly on each outbreath.

THURSDAY: This prayer is adapted from one by the Venerable Thich Nhat Hahn, quoted in the *Oxford Book of Prayer*, OUP, 1985, and acknowledged with thanks.

FRIDAY: The Jesus Prayer comes between two prayers by the compiler and can be incorporated as a refrain in either of them.

SATURDAY: The first prayer is a Christian mantra based on the Lord's Prayer, and is similar in form to the Buddhist 'Om Mane Padmi Hum'. 'Yah' is an almost wordless cry from which the word 'Yahweh' may have originally come, the latter being translated 'the Lord' in the Hebrew Scriptures. 'Abba' is Aramaic for 'Father' and is the word Jesus used. 'Bapu' is a similar Indian word, also used in the prayers on Wednesday. 'Ruach' is Hebrew for 'Spirit', 'Yesu' is almost the same as the Greek 'Iesous', or 'Jesus'.

Of the prayers on p.69, the first is similar to a prayer for world peace, originally composed, I think, by George Appleton, to whom thanks are due. The second and third are by the compiler, and the fourth is inspired by a prayer of the Taizé community.

SUNDAY

OPENING PRAYER AND HYMN

Eternal Spirit,
flow through our being and open our lips,
that our mouths may proclaim your praise
Let us worship the God of Love:
Alleluia, alleluia.

Most glorious Lord of life, that on this day
Didst make thy triumph over death and sin,
And having harrowed hell, didst bring away
Captivity thence captive, us to win:
This joyous day, dear Lord, with joy begin,
And grant that we for whom thou didest die,
Being with thy dear Blood clean washed from sin,
May live for ever in felicity:
And that thy love we weighing worthily,
May likewise love thee for the same again;
And for thy sake, that all like dear didst buy,
With love may one another entertain;
So let us love, dear Love, like as we ought;
Love is the lesson which the Lord us taught.

PSALM 119 [1]

WALKING IN GOD'S PATH

[God's invitation to us is to follow Christ. It is a journey into Love, along a path that is rarely smooth. The Way is rough, the Truth is costly, the Life is sacrificial. The gate through which we are drawn by Love is always narrow.]

The journey	The stony road
The invitation	Follow the Way, the Truth, the Life
The implication	Enter by the narrow gate

> Blessed are those who are honest in their ways,
> who walk in the paths of God's Law.
> Blessed are those who treasure God's Wisdom,
> who seek God with all their heart.
> Those who do no evil deeds
> are those who tread the way of Justice.
> Dear God, you have given command
> that we diligently hold to your Word.
> May my ways be kept steadfast
> on the narrow road of your Love.
> So I shall not be confounded
> while I respect the whole of your Counsel.
> I shall thank you with unfeigned heart
> as I learn to be guided by your Spirit.
> I shall hold fast to your Truths:
> do not utterly abandon me.

PSALM 119 [II]

Delighting in God's Wisdom

[*The path is tough, and, despite boundary marks, we wander from it. We become self-centred; we ignore others on the path. We are constantly invited to love others as Christ has loved us: that degree of love is not easy for it challenges us to bless, pray for, and help those who are hostile to us.*]

The journey	Boundary marks
The invitation	Love one another as I have loved you
The implication	Do good to those who hate you
	Bless those who curse you
	Pray for those who abuse you

How shall the young find their way?
By guarding the boundary of your Word.
With my whole heart I have looked for you:
let me not wander from your Commandment.
Your Truth have I hidden within my heart,
so that I should not fail to love you.
You are blessed indeed, dear God:
teach me your Wisdom.
With my lips I have been telling
of all the Judgements of your mouth.
I have had greater delight in the ways of your Loving
than in all manner of riches.
I will dare to contemplate your Countenance,
and I will deeply respect your Ways.
My delight will be in your Counsel,
and I shall not forget your Word.

PSALM 119 [III]

Longing for God's Justice

[*As travellers into God we need guideposts which can be discerned from within the words of the Gospels. For example, we are blessed when we hunger and thirst for the right relationships longed for by a just God. Only by being faithful to such wisdom will our lives be built on rock.*]

The journey	Guideposts
The invitation	Be faithful to what I have said
The implication	Build on rock

> Deal bountifully with your servant,
> that I may live, and keep your Word.
> Open my eyes that I may see
> the wondrous things of your Law.
> I am a traveller upon earth:
> hide not your Guideposts from me.
> I am consumed with a very fervent desire,
> a longing that I have for your Justice.
> You have rebuked the pride that lurks in me,
> you rescue me when I am lost and astray.
> Take away from me the spirit of scorn,
> hold me fast to the rock of your Truth.
> Keep me from suspicion and hatred:
> rather may I meditate on your Counsel.
> For your Sayings are my delight,
> and they are my counsellors.

PSALM 119 [IV]

Enduring in God's Way

[*When the way is dusty and hot, it is easy to feel weighed down and oppressed. We have then to stop and dig deep in the desert until we discover springs of refreshing water. We also need to learn to receive nourishment from other travellers, as much as in our turn give to them.*]

The journey	Water
The invitation	Let living water flow in you
The implication	Feed the hungry
	Give water to the thirsty

My soul is weighed down like lead:
revive me according to your Word.
When I told you of my ways, you heard me.
Teach me your Wisdom.
Help me to understand the Way of your Love,
and to meditate on the wonders of your Deeds.
My soul droops for very heaviness:
refresh me according to your Promise.
Take from me the way of lying,
and graciously teach me your Truth.
I have chosen the way of faithfulness,
and your Justice is before my eyes.
I cleave to your Law:
let me not be put to shame.
I shall run the way of your Commandment
when you have set my heart at liberty.

MYSTERIES OF GLORY

1 CREATION The earth was without form and void, and darkness was upon the face of the deep; and the Spirit of God was moving over the face of the waters.

2 RESURRECTION Very early on the first day of the week the women went to the tomb when the sun had risen . . . They saw that the stone has been rolled back, and in the tomb a young man said to them, "Do not be amazed; you seek Jesus of Nazareth, who was crucified. He has risen, he is not here; see the place where they laid him."

3 ASCENSION When Jesus had said to the disciples that they would receive the Holy Spirit to be his witnesses to the ends of the earth, he was lifted up from them as they looked, and a cloud took him out of their sight.

4 HOLY SPIRIT Suddenly a sound came from heaven like the rush of a mighty wind, and it filled all the house where they were sitting. And there appeared to them tongues as of fire, distributed and resting on each of them.

5 CONSUMMATION The sufferings of this present time are not worth comparing with the glory that is to be revealed to us. For the creation waits with eager longing for the revealing of the children of God, whose glorious liberty it will attain when set free from bondage and decay.

MYSTERIES OF HOPE

6 THE STRANGER The one with whom Jacob strove all night said to him, "Your name shall no more be called Jacob, for you have striven with God and with men, and have prevailed." The stranger would not give his name, but blessed him. And Jacob called the name of the place Peniel, saying, "I have seen God face to face and yet my life is preserved."

7 THE UNICORN To the one who conquers I will give some of the hidden manna, and I will give a white stone, with a new name written on the stone which no one knows except the one who receives it.

8 THE LAMB Like a lamb that is led to the slaughter, and like a sheep that before its shearers is dumb, so he opened not his mouth.

9 THE EARTH The earth shall be full of the knowledge of God as the waters cover the sea.

10 THE SIGNPOST Jacob woke out of his dream of the ladder between heaven and earth, and said, "Surely the Lord is in this place and I did not know it." And he was afraid, and said, "How awesome is this place! This is none other than the house of God, and this is the gate of heaven." And he took the stone which he had put under his head and set it up for a pillar and poured oil on top of it, and called the name of the place Bethel, the house of God.

PRAYERS

Hail Mary, full of grace, the Lord is with you.
Blessed are you among women,
and blessed is the fruit of your womb, Jesus.
| Holy Mary, Mother of God, pray for us sinners,
now and at the hour of our death.

    Blessed are you, Jesus most holy,
  | dearly beloved, Word become flesh.
    Blessed are you, Jesus the healer,
  | our brother and friend, giver of peace.
    Blessed are you, Jesus, Redeemer,
  | Spirit within us, hope of our glory.

        Yeshua, my Saviour
           Friendship and Love
        Mercy, Healing, Peace.

        Ruach, my Spirit
           Wildness and Warmth
        Wellspring, Living Flame.

        Yahweh, my Creator
           Striving and Pain
        Future, Glory, Joy.

    God of Resurrection –
    Bright Morning Star –
    Lord of the Dance –
    Leap of Faith –
    Stillness of Joy –
        Bless us and all who journey with us,
        this day and always. Amen.

MONDAY

OPENING PRAYER AND HYMN

Eternal Spirit,
flow through our being and open our lips,
that our mouths may proclaim your praise.
Let us worship the God of Love:
Alleluia, alleluia.

How shall I sing that majesty,
Which angels do admire?
Let dust in dust and silence lie,
Sing, sing, ye heavenly choir.
Thousands of thousands stand around
Thy throne, O God most high;
Ten thousand times ten thousand sound
Thy praise; but who am I?

Thy brightness unto them appears,
Whilst I thy footsteps trace;
A sound of God comes to my ears,
But they behold thy face.
They sing because thou art their Sun;
Lord, send a beam on me;
For where heaven is but once begun
There alleluias be.

How great a being, Lord, is thine,
Which doth all beings keep!
Thy knowledge is the only line
To sound so vast a deep.
Thou art a sea without a shore,
A sun without a sphere;
Thy time is now and evermore,
Thy place is everywhere.

PSALM 119 [v]

DESIRING LIFE IN GOD'S SPIRIT

[*We are called simply to follow, but with deep desire and not with reluctance. It is not a path of human cleverness, but of the Spirit of Wisdom. So we are to turn our eyes from envy of others' success, and turn them towards those who are needy.*]

The journey   Following

The invitation   Receive the Holy Spirit

The implication   Give to everyone who asks you

> Teach me, dear God, the Way of your Truth,
> and I shall follow it to the end.
> Give me understanding, and I shall keep your Law,
> I shall keep it with my whole heart.
> Lead me in the path of Wisdom;
> to do your Will is my deepest desire.
> Incline my heart to your Love,
> and not to envious greed.
> Turn away my eyes from vanity,
> and give me life in your Spirit.
> Establish me in your Promise,
> be faithful to those who are in awe of you.
> Take away from me the rejection that I fear,
> for your Justice is good.
> See, my delight is in your Commandment:
> quicken me in the power of your Word.

PSALM 119 [VI]

KEEPING GOD'S WORD

[*To keep on being steadily steadfast in God's Truth even when afraid of the powerful — this is to walk in a sacred manner. It is possible only if we dwell in God's Love. We shall be so delighted in God that we shall not even want to condemn those who would harm us.*]

The journey	Walking
The invitation	Abide in my love
The implication	Judge not and you will not be judged
	Condemn not and you will not be condemned
	Forgive and you will be forgiven

Let your steadfast Love spread over me, dear God,
even your salvation, according to your Promise.
So shall I have an answer for those who taunt me,
for my trust is in your Word.
Take not the Word of your Truth utterly out of my mouth,
for my hope is in your Justice.
So shall I always keep your Law,
for ever and ever the ways of your Love.
And I shall walk at liberty,
glad to fulfil your Commands.
I shall speak of your Wisdom and not be ashamed,
even among the powerful of the earth.
My delight shall be in your Counsel,
which I cherish with joy.
I shall lift up my hands in your Presence,
and listen deep within for your Word.

PSALM 119 [VII]

Remembering God's Promise

[*We go astray from the path. We pursue worldly wealth at others' expense, we despise the weak, we even betray friends. To remember God's Promise to be with us always, to ask that we may embody the Spirit of Christ, to contemplate and treasure Wisdom: only so do we renew our pilgrimage.*]

The journey   Astray

The invitation   Ask in my name

The implication   Do not lay up for yourselves treasure on earth

Remember your Promise to your servant,
in which you have caused me to put my trust.
It is my comfort in time of trouble,
for your Word has given me life.
In pride we despise one another:
may we not shrink from your Law.
Let us remember your Justice, O God,
and we shall be strengthened.
May my anger be cleansed by your Truth,
as I confront betrayal and wrong.
Your Sayings have been my songs
in the house of my pilgrimage.
I have thought upon your Name in the watches of the night,
and I have treasured your Wisdom.
It has been for my blessing,
when I have lived by your Commandment of Love.

MYSTERIES OF JOY

1 ANNUNCIATION The angel Gabriel came to Mary and said, "Hail, O favoured one, the Lord is with you . . . Do not be afraid, for you have found favour with God. And behold, you will conceive in your womb and bear a son, and shall call his name Jesus." . . . And Mary said, "Behold, I am the handmaid of the Lord; let it be to me according to your word."

2 VISITATION Her cousin Elizabeth said to Mary, "Blessed are you among women, and blessed is the fruit of your womb! . . . For when the voice of your greeting came to my ears, the babe in my womb leaped for joy."

3 NATIVITY Mary gave birth to her first-born son and wrapped him in swaddling cloths, and laid him in a manger, because there was no room for them in the inn.

4 PRESENTATION Simeon said to Mary, "Behold, this child is set for the fall and rising of many in Israel, and for a sign that is spoken against (and a sword will pierce through your own soul also), that thoughts out of many hearts may be revealed."

5 PRESENCE IN THE TEMPLE Jesus said to Mary and Joseph, "How is it that you sought me? Did you not know that I must be in my Father's house? . . . And his mother kept all these things in her heart. And Jesus increased in wisdom and in stature, and in favour with God and with all those who knew him.

MYSTERIES OF NATURE

1 MOUNTAIN Sing, O heavens; shout, O depths of the earth; break forth into singing, O mountains, O forest, and every tree of the valleys! For God has come to redeem us, to give us great blessing.

2 FLOWER Consider the lilies of the field, how they grow; they neither toil nor spin; yet I tell you, even Solomon in all his glory was not arrayed like one of these.

3 TREE Your trees O God, are watered abundantly, the cedars of Lebanon which you planted. In them the birds build their nests; the stork has her home in the fir trees.

4 OCEAN Yonder is the sea, great and wide, which teems with things innumerable, living things both small and great. There go the ships, and Leviathan which you did form to sport in it.

5 MOON Creator God, you made the two great lights, the greater light of the sun to rule the day, the lesser light of the moon to rule the night; and you also made the myriad stars.

PRAYERS

Hail Mary, full of grace, the Lord is with you.
Blessed are you among women,
and blessed is the fruit of your womb, Jesus.
Holy Mary, Mother of God, pray for us sinners,
now and at the hour of our death.

> Blessed are you, Jesus most holy,
> dearly beloved, Word made flesh.
> Blessed are you, Jesus the healer,
> our brother and friend, giver of peace.
> Blessed are you, Jesus, Redeemer,
> Spirit within us, hope of our glory.

Dear God, our Creator,
Beloved Companion and Guide upon the Way,
Eternal Spirit within us and beyond us:

Let us honour your name
in lives of costly giving love;

Let us show that we
and all whom we meet
deserve dignity and respect,
for they are your dwelling place
and your home;

Let us share in action
your deep desire for justice and peace
among the peoples of the world;

Let us share our bread with one another,
the bread that you have shared with us;

Let us in the spirit of your forgiving us
make friends with those we've hurt
and failed to love;

Let us overcome our trials and temptations,
our suffering and dying,
in the strength and courage
with which you overcame them too;

Let us in your love
free the world from evil,
transforming darkness into light;

For the whole universe is yours,
and you invite us to be partners
in the work of your creating.

Amen.

So be it.

So will we do it.

TUESDAY

OPENING PRAYER AND HYMN

Eternal Spirit,
flow through our being and open our lips,
that our mouths may proclaim your praise.
Let us worship the God of Love:
Alleluia, alleluia.

> Not a god beyond our reaching,
> High above the bright blue sky,
> But a strong supporting Presence,
> Ground of being, Source of Life.
>
> Not a god of fear and trembling,
> Fire and brimstone from above,
> But the ever-wounded Healer,
> And Refining Fire of Love.
>
> Not the terror-striking spirit
> Of the powers that us enthral,
> But God's Spirit, warm and flowing,
> Melting ice and freeing all.
>
> Not a god of human making,
> Trivial idol of our mind,
> But the God beyond conceiving,
> Destiny of humankind.

PSALM 119 [VIII]

ENJOYING GOD'S PRESENCE

[*We are enlivened and encouraged on the journey by companions —
literally those with whom we eat bread. Even the stranger is to be welcomed
as one who also belongs to God. We are to taste and see the goodness of the
One who gives us living bread.*]

The journey	Companions
The invitation	Eat of the Living Bread
The implication	Welcome the stranger

Dear God, you are my portion for ever:
I have promised to live by your Spirit.
With heart and longing I come into your Presence:
show me your steadfast Love, according to your Word.
I call your Truth to remembrance,
and turn my feet to your Way.
I make haste, and prolong not the time,
that I might keep your Commandments.
The cords of the ungodly ensnare me:
may I not forget your Law.
At midnight I will rise to give you thanks,
because the Judge of all the world acts well.
I am the companion of all who are in awe of you,
who are guided by your Counsel.
The earth, O God, is full of your steadfast Love:
O teach me your Wisdom.

PSALM 119 [ix]

Receiving God's Grace

[*Fortified by God and by one another we journey on. Knowing that we are accepted as we are, we can the more readily accept and forgive others. We have received the gracious and truthful presence of God, far more enriching than all the world's wealth.*]

The journey   On course again

The invitation   Forgive the sins of others

The implication   Forgive to seventy times seven

> Dear God, you have given me grace,
> and so fulfilled your Promise.
> Teach me true understanding and knowledge,
> for I have trusted your Word.
> Before I was afflicted I went astray,
> but now I keep your Counsel.
> You are good and gracious:
> O teach me your Wisdom.
> Through pride I tell lies against my neighbour:
> keep me to your Truth with my whole heart.
> My heart grows fat and gross:
> let my delight be in your Love.
> It is good for me that I have been afflicted,
> that I may learn your Wisdom.
> The Sayings of your mouth are dearer to me
> than thousands of gold and silver pieces.

PSALM 119 [x]

Letting Be in God's Hands

[*We are misled if we think our hard travelling earns us anything as of right. We have to take time to stand still and do nothing, to let go of our concerns, and to let be in God's hands, simply to trust and be thankful.*]

The journey	Standing still
The invitation	To do the work of God is to believe in the One whom God has sent
The implication	Hold on to your life and you will lose it Let go of your life and you will find it

Your hands have made me and fashioned me:
give me understanding that I may know your Mind.
Those who fear you will be glad when they see me,
because I have put my trust in your Word.
I know that your Judgments are right,
that in your faithfulness you have caused me to be troubled.
Let your merciful kindness be my comfort,
according to your Promise to your servant.
Let your loving mercies come to me, that I may live,
for your Love is my delight.
Let my pride be confounded, with its twists of deceit,
and I will meditate on your Wisdom.
Let those who fear you turn to me,
that they may know your Truth.
Let my heart be found in your Counsel,
that I may not be ashamed.

MYSTERIES OF THE NAME OF JESUS

1 YESHUA – SAVIOUR – SALVE It was I who taught Ephraim to walk. I took them up in my arms. But they did not know that I healed them. I led them with cords of compassion, with the bands of love, and I became to them as one who eases the yoke on their jaws. And I bent down to them and fed them.

2 CHRISTOS – ANOINTED – OINTMENT Jesus said, "Why do you trouble the woman? For she has done a beautiful thing to me. For you always have the poor with you, but will not always have me. In pouring this ointment on my body she has done it to prepare me for burial."

3 ELDER BROTHER He became the first-born among many brothers and sisters.

4 TRUE HUMANITY – THE NEW ADAM AND EVE It is written, "The first man Adam became a living being." The last Adam became a life-giving spirit . . . Just as we have borne the image of the man of dust, we shall also bear the image of the man of heaven.

5 LIBERATING LOVER My beloved speaks and says to me, "Arise, my love, my fair one, and come away; for lo, the winter is past, the rain is over and gone. The flowers appear on the earth, the time of singing has come, and the voice of the turtledove is heard in our land."

6 STRIVING PIONEER It was fitting that he, for whom and by whom all things exist, in bringing many sons and daughters to glory, should make the pioneer of their salvation perfect through suffering..

7 HEALER MAKING WHOLE Again Jesus laid his hands on the blind man's eyes, and he looked intently and was restored, and saw everything clearly.

8 PAIN-BEARER He was wounded for our transgressions, he was bruised for our iniquities; upon him was the chastisement that makes us whole, and with his stripes we are healed.

9 BODILY PRESENCE OF GOD In Christ the whole fulness of deity dwells bodily.

10 THOU I Am Who I Am; I Shall Be What I Shall Be . . . Before Abraham Was, I Am.

PRAYERS

Hail Mary, full of grace, the Lord is with you.
Blessed are you among women,
and blessed is the fruit of your womb, Jesus.
Holy Mary, Mother of God, pray for us sinners,
now and at the hour of our death.

> Blessed are you, Jesus most holy,
> dearly beloved, Word become flesh.
> Blessed are you, Jesus the healer,
> our brother and friend, giver of peace.
> Blessed are you, Jesus, Redeemer,
> Spirit within us, hope of our glory

Reaching upwards and yearning,
we adore the One who is beyond us.

Reaching downwards and delving,
we are rooted in our true ground.

Being pruned by confessing the truth,
we enter life by a narrow gate.

Opening our arms wide to welcome our neighbour,
we forgive to seventy times seven.

Reaching backwards into the past,
we absorb what is good and are thankful.

Reaching forwards into the future,
we give of ourselves in trust.

Becoming still in the present,
we rest in the silence of being.

In the presence and power
of divine Love dwelling in me
may I now radiate

> Love
> Compassion
> Joy
> Peace

to those I love and trust . . .

to those who are my enemies . . .

to those of power, influence, decision . . .

to those in trouble and need . . .

to those in prison . . .

to the peacemakers . . .

to the fools for God . . .

to the dying . . .

to those who have died . . .

to all humankind . . .

to all creation . . .

May God give us the covenant of peace
in these our times
and in the fulfilment of time

WEDNESDAY

OPENING PRAYER AND HYMN

Eternal Spirit,
flow through our being and open our lips,
that our mouths may proclaim your praise.
Let us worship the God of Love:
Alleluia, alleluia.

> "There is in God, some say,
> A deep but dazzling darkness . . ."

A word to a young girl but half understood,
The hovering wings of the shadow of God,
The light of the world and sword that shall pierce
   From her deep dark womb.

A birth hardly noticed some way from her home,
A sign in the dark for the outcast who roam,
The faintest of lights from the newest of stars
   In the deep dark cave.

The cold wind of Friday extinguished that light,
Folk grieved that they sank once again in their plight,
His cry pierced the night and they find he is gone
   From the deep dark tomb.

The lanterns of Christmas may point to that star,
Yet spaces between make us still journey far,
Inviting our trust in that long dazzling fall
   Into God's deep dark.

PSALM 119 [xi]

Clinging to God's Faithfulness

[*The vision with which we started out seems to shrivel. Eyesight and insight grow dim. We harm rather than help one another. At best we doggedly endure, clinging to the faithfulness of God who encourages us with Christ's victory over all that would drag us down. Feeling stripped to the bone, we are yet called to clothe one another.*]

The journey	Stumbling
The invitation	Be of good courage: I have overcome the world
The implication	Clothe the naked

I faint with longing for your salvation:
with hope I still cleave to your Word.
My eyes grow dim with watching for your Promise,
saying, When will you comfort me?
For I am like a wineskin shrivelled in the smoke,
yet I do not forget your Wisdom.
How long must your servant endure?
When will you judge those who oppress me?
Yet I too have laid traps for others,
and I have not obeyed your Law.
All your Commandments are true:
and yet we lie to one another.
We have almost made an end of ourselves upon earth:
draw us back who have forsaken your Way.
Quicken me in your loving kindness:
and I shall keep the Counsel of your Spirit.

PSALM 119 [xii]

Trusting in God's Purpose

[*In the very midst of constriction the vision is renewed. Sustained by the eternity and reliability and promised fulfilment of the purposes of God's Love, nourished by the blood-red wine of the very life of God, we continue to walk with our burdens, simply following the Way.*]

The journey	Vision
The invitation	Live in the True Vine
The implication	Take up your cross and follow me

Dear God, your eternal Word of Love
endures for ever in the universe.
Your Truth stands fast from one generation to another:
you have laid the foundations of the earth, and it abides.
In fulfilment of your Purpose it continues to this very day,
for all things serve you.
If my delight had not been in your Wisdom,
I should have perished in my trouble.
I shall never forget your Truths,
for with them you have given me life.
I belong to you, save me,
for I have sought your Counsel.
Many are the traps that could destroy me,
but I will meditate on your Law.
I see that all things come to an end,
but your Commandment is exceeding broad.

PSALM 119 [XIII]

LOVING GOD'S TRUTH

[*We miss our way if we do not become childlike in our trust and delight in the tastiness of God's gifts. Even the commandment to love in a tough, enduring, non-possessive way is as honey to our deepest selves. We come to relish the Wisdom, Counsel, and Truths of God.*]

The journey   Honey

The invitation   If you love me keep my commandment

The implication   Become like children

> Dear God, how I love your Wisdom:
> all day long is my study in it.
> Your Counsel makes me wiser than my adversaries,
> for it is always in my heart.
> I have more understanding than my teachers,
> for I meditate on your Word.
> I am wiser than the aged
> because I keep your Truths in my heart.
> I hold back my feet from evil ways,
> that I may obey your will.
> When I do not turn aside from your Way,
> I know that you are my Guide.
> How tasty are your Sayings to my mouth,
> sweeter than honey to my tongue.
> Through your guidance I learn understanding:
> therefore I hate all evil ways.

MYSTERIES OF PEOPLE HEALED AND CHALLENGED

1 THE PARALYZED MAN Through an opening in the roof his friends let down the pallet on which the paralyzed man lay. And when Jesus saw their faith, he said to the paralyzed man, "My son, your sins are forgiven . . . Rise, take up your pallet, and go home."

2 THE CENTURION AND HIS SLAVE-BOY A centurion had a slave who was dear to him and who was ill. He sent friends to Jesus with this message: "Lord, do not trouble yourself, for I am not worthy to have you come under my roof . . . but say the word, and let my servant be healed." Jesus marvelled, "Not even in Israel have I found such faith."

3 THE WOMAN WITH A HAEMORRHAGE The woman touched the fringe of Jesus' garment; and immediately her flow of blood ceased. Jesus perceived that power had gone out from him, and the woman came trembling and declared what had happened.

4 THE TENTH LEPER One of the ten lepers who had been cleansed, when he saw that he was healed, turned back, praising God with a loud voice; he fell on his face at Jesus' feet, giving him thanks. Now he was a Samaritan.

5 THE SYROPHOENICIAN WOMAN She begged Jesus to cast the demon out of her daughter and said to Jesus that even if it is not right to take the children's bread and throw it to the dogs, even the dogs eat the crumbs from under the table.

6 THE LAME MAN A lame man had been ill thirty-eight years, with no one to put him into the pool of Bethzatha when the water was troubled. Jesus said to him, "Do you want to be healed?".

7 THE MOTHER AND BROTHERS OF JESUS When his mother and his brothers came to see him, Jesus looked round on those who sat about him and said, "Here are my mother and brothers! Whoever does the will of God is my brother, and sister, and mother".

8 THE WOMAN OF SAMARIA Jesus, a Jewish man, coming to a well, had asked a Samaritan woman for a drink. He talked with her of living water and of worship in spirit and truth, and revealed her to herself. She went into the city and said to the people, "Come, see a man who told me all that I ever did. Can this be the Christ?".

9 ZACCHEUS Jesus invited himself to the home of the tax collector, who responded, "I give half of my goods to the poor; and if I have defrauded anyone of anything, I restore it fourfold".

10 THE LAWYER A lawyer who came to Jesus one day knew well the heart of the law: loving God and loving neighbour. Wanting to know who was his neighbour, he was told the story of the Samaritan tending the man who had been robbed, and realized that he had to follow the example of the one his countrymen would despise. "Go and do likewise," said Jesus.

PRAYERS

Hail Mary, full of grace, the Lord is with you.
Blessed are you among women,
and blessed is the fruit of your womb, Jesus.
Holy Mary, Mother of God, pray for us sinners,
now and at the hour of our death.

> Blessed are you, Jesus most holy,
> dearly beloved, Word made flesh.
> Blessed are you, Jesus the healer,
> our brother and friend, giver of peace.
> Blessed are you, Jesus, Redeemer,
> Spirit within us, hope of our glory.

>> Bapu dear God
>> may your Name
>> be well honoured

>> Bapu dear God
>> may your reign
>> spread among us

>> Bapu dear God
>> may your will
>> be well done

>> at all times
>> in all places

>> Give us today
>> what we need for today

>> Forgive us our sins
>> as we forgive those
>> who sin against us

Let us not fail
in time of our testing

Spare us from trials
too great to endure

Free us from the grip
of all evil powers

For yours is the reign
the power and the glory
the victory of love
in time and eternity
world without end

May the God of peace and love and faith
transform the universe to glory. Amen.

THURSDAY

OPENING PRAYER AND HYMN

Eternal Spirit,
flow through our being and open our lips,
that our mouths may proclaim your praise.
Let us worship the God of Love:
Alleluia, alleluia.

> In the heart of Love, begotten
> Ere the world from chaos rose,
> You are Alpha: from that Fountain
> All that is and has been flows:
> You are Omega, of all things
> Yet to come the mystic Close:
> *Evermore and evermore.*
>
> You became our mortal body,
> Frail and feeble, doomed to die,
> That the race from dust created
> Might not perish utterly,
> For without your grace we wither
> And decay, in hell to lie:
>
> O how blest is Mary, Mother,
> She the first who new believed,
> Brought to birth the world's salvation,
> By the Holy Ghost conceived;
> And the Babe, the True Redeemer,
> In her loving arms received:
>
> Sing, O earth and seas, God's praises,
> Sun and storms and sounding shore,
> Streams and forest, faithful people,
> Day and night the Christ adore,
> Born for us and all creation
> Through a Love for ever sure:

PSALM 119 [XIV]

BEING GUIDED BY GOD'S LIGHT

[*The Way becomes obscure, but there is sufficient light once our eyes are accustomed to the dark. We may not realize that we are being guided in a particular direction, but the shepherd's crook is kindly prompting. We may be troubled, but an imperceptible inclination of the heart in prayer is all that is needed for our calming.*]

The journey   Lantern in the dark

The invitation   Let the Good Shepherd guide

The implication   Pray simply

Your Word is a lantern to my feet,
a light searching out all my ways.
I have sworn, and am steadfastly purposed
to keep the Way of your Justice.
I am troubled beyond measure:
give me life, dear God, according to your Promise.
Accept my offerings of praise,
and teach me your Truths.
My life is always in your hand,
and I do not forget your Law.
The ungodly have laid a snare for me:
may I not swerve from your Commandment.
Your wisdom have I claimed as my heritage for ever,
it is the very joy of my heart.
I incline my heart to your Counsel,
always, even to the end.

PSALM 119 [xv]

BRINGING EVIL TO GOD'S LOVE

[*We try to avoid the refining fire of God's truth. We resist the pruning of our self-centredness. We are unfaithful to our promises, we are cunning in our self-deceits, we become weighed down with our vain pursuit of earthly security. Even while hating hypocrisy, we practise it. Only through the astringent love of God will our greedy and inordinate desires cease, our lust for possessions fade.*]

The journey   Refining fire

The invitation   Be pruned, and be fruitful

The implication   Do not look lustfully

I hate all doublemindedness and hypocrisy,
but your Law do I love.
You are my defence and my shield,
and my trust is in your Word.
Away from me, all desire to do evil:
I will keep the Commandment of my God.
Uphold me according to your Promise, and I shall live:
let me not be disappointed of my hope.
Support me, and I shall be safe:
my delight shall ever be in your Wisdom.
Relentlessly expose my unfaithfulness;
may my cunning be in vain.
Rake out ungodliness from me like dross,
for I desire your refining Truths.
My flesh trembles in awe of you,
and I am afraid of your Judgments.

PSALM 119 [XVI]

SERVING GOD'S WILL

[*As servants of the will of God, called to love God's wisdom as a precious jewel, we begin to discover that indeed possessions are of no account. We appreciate the wealth that comes to us through enjoying the smallest and simplest acts of kindness, given and received. No earthly greatness could ever compensate for such true treasure.*]

The journey	Possessions of no account
The invitation	Wash one another's feet
The implication	Whoever would be great among you must be your servant

I have done what is just and right:
do not give me over into the hands of my oppressors.
make your servant delight in all that is good,
that the proud may do me no wrong.
My eyes waste away with looking for your salvation,
for the fulfilment of your righteous Promise.
Embrace your servant in your steadfast Love,
and teach me your Wisdom.
I am your servant: give me understanding
that I may know your Counsel.
It is high time that you acted, O God,
for your Law is being destroyed.
How I would come to love your Commandments
beyond all gold and precious stones.
Therefore I direct my steps in your Way,
and all false steps I utterly abhor.

MYSTERIES OF OBEDIENCE

1 BAPTISM When Jesus was baptized, he went up immediately from the water, and the heavens were opened and he saw the Spirit of God descending like a dove and alighting on him; and a voice from heaven said, "This is my beloved Son, with whom I am well pleased."

2 TEMPTATION "Command these stones to become bread" – "The human race shall not live by bread alone but by the living Word of God." "Throw yourself down from the pinnacle of the Temple" – "You shall not put the Lord your God to the test." "I will give you all the kingdoms of the world and their glory if you will worship me" – "You shall worship God alone."

3 TRANSFIGURATION Jesus was transfigured before Peter, James, and John, and his face shone like the sun, and his clothing became white as light.

4 ANOINTING Jesus said of the woman, "In pouring this ointment on my body she has done it to prepare me for burial."

5 SUPPER Now as they were eating, Jesus took bread, and blessed, and broke it, and gave it to his disciples and said, "Take, eat; this is my body." And he took a cup of wine, and when he had given thanks he gave it to them, saying, "Drink of this, all of you; for this is my blood of the covenant, which is poured out for many for the forgiveness of sins."

MYSTERIES OF DISCIPLESHIP

6 MARY When the shepherds had seen Mary and Joseph and the babe lying in a manger, they made known the saying which had been told them concerning the child. But Mary kept all these things, pondering them in her heart.

7 PETER The cock crowed a second time and Peter remembered how Jesus had said to him, "Before the cock crows twice, you will deny me three times." And he broke down and wept bitterly.

8 JAMES AND JOHN Jesus saw James the son of Zebedee and John his brother, who were in their boat mending the nets. And immediately he called them; and they left their father Zebedee in the boat with the hired servants, and followed him.

9 JUDAS Lying close to the breast of Jesus, the beloved disciple asked him, "Lord, who is it that will betray you?" Jesus answered, "It is he to whom I shall give this morsel when I have dipped it." He gave it to Judas. Satan entered him. Jesus said to him, "What you are going to do, do quickly. He immediately went out; and it was night.

10 LAZARUS Jesus cried with a loud voice, "Lazarus, come forth." The dead man came out of the tomb, his hands and feet bound with bandages, and his face wrapped with a cloth. Jesus said to them, "Loose him, and let him go."

PRAYERS

Hail Mary, full of grace, the Lord is with you.
Blessed are you among women,
and blessed is the fruit of your womb, Jesus.
Holy Mary, Mother of God, pray for us sinners,
now and at the hour of our death.

> Blessed are you, Jesus most holy,
> dearly beloved, Word become flesh.
> Blessed are you, Jesus the healer,
> our brother and friend, giver of peace.
> Blessed are you, Jesus, Redeemer,
> Spirit within us, hope of our glory.

> Let us be truly with one another,
> in physical presence and in mind's eye

Silence

Let us pay attention to our breathing

Silence

Let us be relaxed

Silence

Let us be at peace within ourselves

Silence

Let us accept that we are profoundly loved
and need never be afraid

Silence

Let us be aware of the source of being
that is common to all human beings
and to all living creatures

Silence

Let us be filled with the presence
of the Great Compassion,
towards ourselves
and towards all living beings

Silence

Realizing that we are all nourished
from the same source of life
may we so live that others be not deprived
of air, food, shelter, or the chance to live

Silence

Let us pray that we ourselves cease to be
a cause of suffering to one another

Silence

With humility let us pray for
the spreading of peace
in our hearts and on earth

Silence

May God kindle in us
the fire of love
to bring us alive
and give warmth to the world

FRIDAY

OPENING PRAYER AND HYMN

Eternal Spirit,
flow through our being and open our lips,
that our mouths may proclaim your praise.
Let us worship the God of Love:
Alleluia, alleluia.

> Sing, my tongue, the glorious battle,
> Sing the last, the dread affray;
> O'er the Cross, the Victor's trophy,
> Sound the high triumphal lay,
> How, the pains of death enduring,
> Earth's Redeemer won the day.
>
> Faithful Cross! above all other,
> One and only noble Tree!
> None in foliage, none in blossom,
> None in fruit thy peer may be;
> Beauteous wood and radiant iron!
> Goodly weight is hung on thee!
>
> Bend thy boughs, O Tree of Glory!
> Thy too rigid sinews bend;
> And awhile the stubborn hardness,
> Which thy birth bestowed, suspend;
> And the gracious heavenly Monarch
> Gently on thine arms extend.
>
> Praise now be to our Creator,
> Praise to our Redeemer too,
> Praise and honour to the Spirit,
> For the Tree that mighty grew:
> Praise to God with love and glory
> From the universe is due.

PSALM 119 [XVII]

Rejoicing in God's Love

[*God's Love is reliable, steadfast, constant. In that knowledge we can walk firmly, freed from the weight of oppression, with a light step. Even in frightening places, it is as if we are already in the safety of the sheepfold. Living in the spirit of that freedom, we are more able to draw alongside those who are constricted by illness or imprisonment.*]

The journey	Burdens fall away
The invitation	Come in by the Door of the Sheepfold
The implication	Visit the sick and those in prison

Your steadfast Love is wonderful:
therefore I treasure your Wisdom.
When your Word goes forth
it gives light and understanding to the simple.
I opened my mouth and drew in my breath,
for my delight was in your Counsel.
Look upon me and show me kindness,
as is your joy for those who love your Name.
Keep my steps steady in your Word,
and so shall no wickedness get dominion over me.
Relieve me from the weight of oppression,
and so I shall keep your Commandments.
Show the light of your face upon your servant,
and teach me your Way.
My eyes shed streams of sorrow
because folk heed not your Promise.

PSALM 119 [XVIII]

Hungry For God's Justice

[*Freed from the weight of worldly expectation and possessions, humbled and poor, even, like a grain of wheat, dying unnoticed, the followers of the Way are the only ones who can know what it would be like to see God's justice, God's commonwealth, established on earth. They cry with yearning to see right prevail. They strive to make it so.*]

The journey   Humbled and poor

The invitation   Let the grain of wheat fall into the earth and die

The implication   Yearn and strive to see right prevail

You are righteous, O God,
and your Judgments are true.
The Ways that you have commanded
are just and true.
My zeal has consumed me
because my enemies have forgotten your Words.
Your Promise has been well tested,
and your servant loves and delights in it.
I am small, and of no reputation,
yet I do not forget your Wisdom.
Your righteousness is an everlasting righteousness,
and your Law is the Truth.
Trouble and heaviness have taken hold of me,
yet my delight is in your Justice.
The righteousness of your Will is eternal:
give me understanding, and I shall live.

PSALM 119 [XIX]

URGENTLY NEEDING GOD'S GUIDANCE

[*Nevertheless, it is not easy to keep our sense of spiritual direction. We are easily misled and we have to face the malice of the frightened. We shall lie awake at night, seeking to settle our hearts and wills on God. We shall urgently pray for guidance in the day. We may be given the gift of God's peace, but we shall do well to strive with our enemies sooner rather than later.*]

The journey   Awake at night

The invitation   Receive my gift of peace

The implication   Make friends quickly with your adversary

> I call with my whole heart:
> hear me, O God, I will keep your Commandments.
> Urgently do I cry to you:
> help me, and I shall follow your Way.
> Early in the morning do I cry out to you,
> for in your Word is my trust.
> My eyes are awake in the watches of the night,
> that I might meditate on your Promise.
> Hear my voice according to your steadfast Love,
> quicken me, in fulfilment of your Will.
> They draw near who persecute me with malice:
> they are far from your Law.
> But you, O God, are near at hand:
> for all your Counsel is true.
> Long since have I known of your Wisdom,
> that you have grounded it for ever.

MYSTERIES OF SORROW

1 THE AGONY IN THE GARDEN Jesus began to be greatly distressed and troubled, and said to his disciples, "My soul is very sorrowful, even to death." And he prayed that if it were possible the hour might pass from him. "Abba, Father, all things are possible to thee; remove this cup from me; yet not what I will, but what thou wilt."

2 THE SCOURGING Then Pilate took Jesus and scourged him.

3 THE CROWN OF THORNS The soldier plaited a crown of thorns and put it on Jesus' head, and arrayed him in a purple robe; they came up to him and said, "Hail, King of the Jews!" and struck him with their hands.

4 THE CARRYING OF THE CROSS So they took Jesus, and he went out, bearing his own cross, to the place called the place of a skull, which in Hebrew is called Golgotha.

5 THE CRUCIFIXION And when the sixth hour had come, there was darkness over the whole land until the ninth hour. And at the ninth hour Jesus cried with a loud voice, "My God, my God, why hast thou forsaken me?" . . . And Jesus gave a loud cry, and breathed his last.

MYSTERIES OF DESTRUCTION

1 SWORD From the mouth of one like a son of man issued a sharp two-edged sword . . . Let him who has no sword sell his cloak and buy one.

2 BOMB Behold, the Lord will lay waste the earth and make it desolate, and he will twist its surface and scatter its inhabitants . . . The earth mourns and withers . . . and the heavens languish together with the earth.

3 FLAMES Repent, lest my wrath go forth like fire, and burn with none to quench it, because of the evil of your doings.

4 CITY Jesus said to his disciples, "Do you see these great buildings? There will not be left one stone upon another, that will not be thrown down."

5 FIST You fast only to quarrel and to fight and to hit with wicked fist. Fasting like yours this day will not make your voice heard in God's presence.

PRAYERS

Hail Mary, full of grace, the Lord is with you.
Blessed are you among women,
and blessed is the fruit of your womb, Jesus.
Holy Mary, Mother of God, pray for us sinners,
now and at the hour of our death.

> Blessed are you, Jesus most holy,
> dearly beloved, Word become flesh.
> Blessed are you, Jesus the healer,
> our brother and friend, giver of peace.
> Blessed are you, Jesus, Redeemer,
> Spirit within us, hope of our glory.

We confess those things within us which make for war:

> envy . . .
> greed . . .
> fear . . .
> prejudice . . .
> self-hatred . . .
> ignorance . . .
> laziness . . .
> pride . . .
> lust for power . . .
> suspicion of the stranger . . .

> LORD JESUS CHRIST
> SON OF THE LIVING GOD
> HAVE MERCY UPON ME
> A SINNER

For the hungry and the overfed . . .
May we have enough

For the mourners and the mockers . . .
May we laugh together

For the victims and the oppressors . . .
May we share power wisely

For the peacemakers and the warmongers . . .
May clear truth and stern love lead us to harmony

For the silenced and the propagandists . . .
May we speak our own words in truth

For the unemployed and the overworked . . .
May our impress on the earth be kindly and creative

For the troubled and the sleek . . .
May we live together as wounded healers

For the homeless and the cosseted . . .
May our homes be simple, warm, and welcoming

For the vibrant and the dying . . .
May we all die to live

SATURDAY

OPENING PRAYER AND HYMN

Eternal Spirit,
flow through our being and open our lips,
that our mouths may proclaim your praise.
Let us worship the God of Love:
Alleluia, alleluia.

Come, my Way, my Truth, my Life:
Such a Way, as gives us breath;
Such a Truth, as ends all strife;
Such a Life, as killeth death.

Come, my Light, my Feast, my Strength:
Such a Light, as shows a feast;
Such a Feast, as mends in length;
Such a Strength, as makes his guest.

Come, my Joy, my Love, my Heart:
Such a Joy, as none can move;
Such a Love, as none can part;
Such a Heart, as joys in love.

PSALM 119 [xx]

CHERISHING GOD'S COMMAND

[*Not one of us can plead innocence or perfection. There is great contrast between our unfaithfulness and the steadfast love of God. This is painful truth. Only by immersing ourselves in God's Love, only by sharing the cup of affliction which was drained to the full by the only One who was indeed whole, can we be given the life that we desire. On the way we have to deny ourselves much of what we now hold dear.*]

The journey	Aware of painful truth
The invitation	Drink the Cup
The implication	Deny yourself

> Look on my affliction and deliver me;
> may I not forget your Law.
> Plead my cause and redeem me:
> give me life according to your Word.
> Salvation is far from my wickedness,
> when I have no regard for your Commandments.
> Great is your loving kindness, dear God:
> give me life, for such is your joy and delight.
> There are many who trouble me, my adversaries:
> may I not swerve from your Way.
> It grieves me to see our unfaithfulness
> when we ignore all that you promise.
> Consider how I cherish your Wisdom:
> give me life, according to your steadfast Love.
> Your Word is eternally true,
> and your Justice stands fast for ever.

PSALM 119 [XXI]

Standing Firm in God's Counsel

[*If we keep to the Way shown to us, we shall discover the treasures of the Wisdom of God — Love, Truth, Peace, Saving Health, Justice. We are invited to trust and not be faithless, to open all the devices of our locked hearts to God. Then we shall be at peace, be able to absorb and reconcile conflicts, and be makers of peace.*]

The journey Treasure discovered

The invitation Be not faithless but believing

The implication Be a maker of peace

> The powerful oppress me without cause,
> but my heart stands firm in awe of your Word.
> I rejoice in your Love
> more than one who finds great spoils.
> As for lies. I hate and abhor them,
> but your Law do I love.
> Seven times a day do I praise you
> because of the Justice of your Way.
> Great is the peace of those who treasure your Wisdom:
> nothing can make them stumble.
> I have looked for your saving health,
> and followed your Counsel.
> My whole being holds fast to your Justice,
> which I love and long for exceedingly.
> Guide me in the path of your Truth,
> all the ways of my heart are open before you.

PSALM 119 [XXII]

Praising God's Salvation

[*The journey is through a labyrinth. We find our way to our true home by the thinnest of threads. Like bewildered sheep we lose our way in cul-de-sacs of the maze. If we have been found there by the 'angels' of God, then we in turn can at times can be a 'presence' of God to others who are confused. In dark and hidden places we can still give, and pray, and fast. And in the end we shall be brought home rejoicing in the God who saves, in and through and beyond our hopes and fears.*]

The journey	Home through the labyrinth
The invitation	Feed my sheep
The implication	Give secretly
	Pray secretly
	Fast secretly

Let my cry come to your ears, dear God:
give me understanding, according to your Word.
See the labyrinth of my ways:
deliver me, according to your Promise.
My lips shall tell of your praise,
for you show me the path of Wisdom.
My tongue shall sing of your Love
and praise your Justice to the skies.
Let your hand guide me,
steady me with the Counsel of your Spirit.
I have longed for your saving health, O God,
and in your Truth is my delight.
Let me live, that I may praise you:
let your Love and your Justice help me.
I have gone astray like a sheep that is lost:
seek your servant, and bring me home rejoicing.

MYSTERIES OF GRACE

1 WINE I am the vine, you are the branches. If you abide in me, and I in you, you will bear much fruit, for apart from me you can do nothing . . . The wine that gladdens the human heart . . . The wine that is the Blood of Christ.

2 WATER If you drink the water that I shall give you, you will never thirst: the water that I shall give you will become in you a living spring that wells up to eternal life.

3 BREAD I am the bread of life; if you come to me you will not hunger; if you believe in me, you will not thirst . . . The bread that is the Body of Christ.

4 LIGHT I am the light of the world; if you follow me you will not walk in darkness, but you will have the light of life.

5 LIFE I am the resurrection and the life; if you believe in me, though you die, yet shall you live: whoever lives and believes in me will never die.

MYSTERIES OF FEELING

1 ANGER Jesus drove out those who bought and sold in the temple, and said to them, "Is it not written, 'My house shall be called a house of prayer for all nations?' But you have made it a den of robbers."

2 GRIEF Jesus asked, "Where have you laid Lazarus?" The Jews said to him, "Lord, come and see." Jesus wept. So they said, "See how he loved him."

3 FEAR Being in an agony Jesus prayed more earnestly, and his sweat became like great drops of blood falling down upon the ground.

4 LOVE The man said, "Teacher, all these commandments I have observed from my youth." And Jesus looking upon him loved him, and said, "You lack one thing: go, sell what you have, and give to the poor, and you will have treasure in heaven; and come, follow me." At that saying his face fell, and he went away sorrowful; for he had great possessions.

5 JOY "Bring the fatted calf and kill it, and let us eat and make merry; for this my son was dead, and is alive again, was lost, and is found."

PRAYERS

Hail Mary, full of grace, the Lord is with you.
Blessed are you among women,
and blessed is the fruit of your womb, Jesus.
Holy Mary, Mother of God, pray for us sinners,
now and at the hour of our death.

> Blessed are you, Jesus most holy,
> dearly beloved, Word become flesh.
> Blessed are you, Jesus the healer,
> our brother and friend, giver of peace.
> Blessed are you, Jesus, Redeemer,
> Spirit within us, hope of our glory.

```
YAH   ABBA    YESU   YAH
YAH   BAPU    YESU   YAH
YAH   RUACH   YESU   YAH
YAH   ABBA    YESU   FEED
YAH   BAPU    YESU   GIVE
YAH   RUACH   YESU   FREE
YAH   ABBA    YESU   YAH
YAH   BAPU    YESU   YAH
YAH   RUACH   YESU   YAH
```

> O God of many names
> Lover of all peoples
> we pray for peace
> in our hearts and homes
> in our nations and our world
> the peace of your will
> the peace of our need

Dear Christ, our Friend and our Guide,
Pioneer through the shadow of death,
passing through darkness to make it light,
be our companion that we may fear no evil,
and bring us to life and to glory.

> O God of peace and justice,
> of holiness and of love,
> knit us together in mind and flesh,
> in feeling and in spirit,
> and make us one,
> ready for the Great Day,
> the fulfilment of all our hopes,
> and the glory of Jesus Christ.

Keep us in the spirit of joy and simplicity and mercy.
Bless us and those you have entrusted to us,
in and through Jesus Christ our Saviour. Amen.

Also by JIM COTTER
and available from Cairns Publications

Prayer at Night: A Book for the Darkness

Prayer in the Day: A Book of Mysteries
[*Standard edition, with drawings by Peter Pelz*]

Prayer in the Morning: A Book for Day's Beginning

Healing – more or less

What Price Healing in a Time of Epidemic?

Pleasure, Pain and Passion

Good Fruits

No Thank You, I'm 1662:
Cartoons at the Giving of the Peace
[*Drawings by Stuart Yerrell*]